THIS BOOK

BELONGS TO

....

....

I can't tell you how grateful I am that you decided to read my book. My most heartfelt thanks that you took time out of your life to choose my work and I hope you find benefit within these pages.

There are so many books available today that offer similar content so that makes it even more humbling that you decided to buying mine.

Tell me what you thought! I am eager to hear your opinion and ideas on what you read as are others who are looking for a good book to buy. Leave a review on Amazon.com so others can benefit from your wisdom!

With much thanks.

Table of Contents

SUMMARY

The Rich History of Kumihimo: Kumihimo, a traditional Japanese braiding technique, has a rich and fascinating history that spans centuries. The word "kumihimo" itself translates to "gathered threads" in Japanese, which perfectly describes the process of intertwining multiple strands of thread or yarn to create intricate and beautiful braids.

The origins of kumihimo can be traced back to ancient Japan, where it was primarily used for practical purposes such as securing armor and tying up samurai's hair. However, over time, kumihimo evolved into a highly regarded art form, with braids becoming more elaborate and decorative. It was during the Heian period (794-1185) that kumihimo truly flourished, as it became an essential accessory for the aristocracy.

During this period, kumihimo braids were not only used for practical purposes but also as a symbol of status and wealth. The more intricate and complex the braid, the higher the social standing of the individual wearing it. Kumihimo braids were often adorned with precious metals, gemstones, and even pearls, making them highly coveted and sought after.

The techniques and patterns used in kumihimo were closely guarded secrets, passed down from generation to generation within specific families or guilds. These skilled artisans would spend years perfecting their craft, mastering the art of manipulating the threads to create stunning and unique designs. The knowledge and expertise required to create these braids were considered invaluable, and the artisans who possessed this skill were highly respected in society.

Kumihimo continued to evolve and adapt throughout the centuries, with different regions in Japan developing their own distinct styles and techniques. For example, the Yatsu-gumi style, originating from Kyoto, is known for its intricate patterns and use of multiple colors. On the other hand, the Kongoh-gumi style, originating from the Kanto region, is characterized by its simplicity and use of thicker threads.

In modern times, kumihimo has gained international recognition and popularity. It is no longer limited to Japan, as people from all over the world have embraced this ancient art form. Kumihimo braids are now used in various applications, including jewelry making, home decor, and even fashion accessories.

Today, there are numerous kumihimo workshops and classes available, allowing individuals to learn and practice this traditional craft.

The Modern Revival of Kumihimo: The modern revival of Kumihimo, a traditional Japanese braiding technique, has gained significant popularity in recent years. This ancient art form, which dates back to the 7th century, involves the intricate weaving of colorful threads to create stunning and intricate patterns. While Kumihimo has been practiced for centuries in Japan, it is now being embraced by artisans and crafters all over the world.

One of the reasons for the resurgence of Kumihimo is its versatility. This braiding technique can be used to create a wide range of items, from jewelry and accessories to home decor and clothing embellishments. The possibilities are endless, and artists are constantly finding new and innovative ways to incorporate Kumihimo into their work.

Another factor contributing to the modern revival of Kumihimo is the accessibility of materials and tools. In the past, the supplies needed for Kumihimo were often difficult to find outside of Japan. However, with the rise of online shopping and the global marketplace, it is now easier than ever to source high-quality threads, beads, and findings for Kumihimo projects. Additionally, there are now specialized tools available, such as Kumihimo disks and marudai (a traditional braiding stand), that make the process more accessible to beginners.

The resurgence of Kumihimo can also be attributed to the growing interest in traditional crafts and handmade goods. In a world dominated by mass-produced items, many people are seeking out unique and personalized pieces that reflect their individuality. Kumihimo offers a way to create one-of-a-kind items that are not only beautiful but also carry a sense of history and tradition.

Furthermore, the revival of Kumihimo has been fueled by the sharing of knowledge and techniques through workshops, classes, and online communities. Crafters are coming together to learn from each other, exchange ideas, and showcase their creations. This sense of community and collaboration has helped to spread the love for Kumihimo and inspire others to give it a try.

In conclusion, the modern revival of Kumihimo is a testament to the enduring beauty and appeal of this ancient Japanese braiding technique. Its versatility, accessibility, and connection to tradition have made it a favorite among artisans and crafters worldwide. Whether you are a seasoned crafter or a beginner looking to explore a new hobby, Kumihimo offers a world of creative possibilities waiting to be discovered.

Kumihimo in Contemporary Craft: Kumihimo, a traditional Japanese braiding technique, has found its place in contemporary craft as a versatile and innovative art form. With its origins dating back to the Heian period (794-1185), Kumihimo has evolved over centuries, adapting to changing trends and styles. Today, it is not only a popular craft in Japan but has also gained recognition and appreciation worldwide.

The technique of Kumihimo involves the interlacing of multiple strands of thread or cord to create intricate and decorative braids. Traditionally, Kumihimo was used to create functional cords for various purposes such as tying kimono sashes (obi) or securing armor. However, in contemporary craft, Kumihimo has transcended its utilitarian origins and has become a medium for artistic expression.

Contemporary artists and crafters have embraced Kumihimo as a means to explore color, texture, and pattern. The technique allows for endless possibilities in terms of design, as different combinations of threads and cords can be used to create unique and visually striking braids. From vibrant and bold color palettes to subtle and delicate gradients, Kumihimo offers a wide range of artistic choices.

In addition to its aesthetic appeal, Kumihimo also offers a meditative and therapeutic experience for both the maker and the viewer. The repetitive and rhythmic motions involved in the braiding process can be calming and soothing, allowing the artist to enter a state of flow. This aspect of Kumihimo has made it a popular craft for relaxation and stress relief.

Contemporary crafters have also pushed the boundaries of Kumihimo by experimenting with different materials and techniques. While traditional Kumihimo uses silk threads or cords made from natural fibers, contemporary artists have incorporated unconventional materials such as wire, beads, and even recycled materials into their braids. This fusion of traditional and modern elements adds a unique and contemporary twist to the craft.

Furthermore, Kumihimo has also found its place in the world of fashion and accessories. Contemporary designers have incorporated Kumihimo braids into jewelry, handbags, and even clothing, adding a touch of elegance and sophistication to their creations. The versatility of Kumihimo allows it to be adapted to various styles and aesthetics, making it a popular choice for both traditional and contemporary fashion.

In conclusion, Kumihimo has successfully made its transition from a traditional Japanese craft to a contemporary art form.

Understanding Kumihimo Discs and Looms: Kumihimo is a traditional Japanese braiding technique that has been practiced for centuries. It involves the use of a disc or a loom to create intricate and beautiful braids. Understanding the different types of Kumihimo discs and looms is essential for anyone interested in learning this art form.

Kumihimo discs are circular tools that are used to hold the threads in place while braiding. They are typically made of foam or plastic and have slots or notches around the edge. These slots are used to guide the threads and create different patterns and designs. The number of slots on a Kumihimo disc can vary, with some discs having as few as eight slots and others having up to 64 slots. The number of slots determines the complexity of the braid that can be created.

To use a Kumihimo disc, the threads are first divided into different groups and then placed into the slots. The threads are then moved in a specific order, following a pattern or design, to create the desired braid. The disc is rotated as the threads are moved, which helps to keep the tension even and ensures that the braid is uniform. The braiding process is repeated until the desired length of the braid is achieved.

Kumihimo looms, on the other hand, are rectangular tools that are used to create wider and more complex braids. They consist of a frame with pegs or slots that hold the threads in place. The number of pegs or slots on a Kumihimo loom can vary, with some looms having as few as four pegs and others having up to 32 pegs. The number of pegs determines the width and complexity of the braid that can be created.

To use a Kumihimo loom, the threads are first divided into different groups and then wrapped around the pegs or placed into the slots. The threads are then moved in a specific order, following a pattern or design, to create the desired braid. The loom is rotated as the threads are moved, which helps to keep the tension even and ensures that the braid is uniform. The braiding process is repeated until the desired length of the braid is achieved.

Both Kumihimo discs and looms offer different advantages and can be used to create a wide variety of braids. Discs are generally more portable and easier to use for beginners, while looms allow for more complex designs and wider braids.

Choosing the Right Kumihimo Cord: When it comes to choosing the right Kumihimo cord, there are several factors to consider. Kumihimo is a traditional Japanese braiding technique that uses cords to create intricate and beautiful designs. The cord you choose will greatly impact the final look and feel of your project, so it's important to make an informed decision.

One of the first things to consider is the material of the cord. Kumihimo cords can be made from a variety of materials, including silk, nylon, cotton, and satin. Each material has its own unique characteristics and will produce a different result. Silk cords, for example, are known for their smooth and luxurious feel, while nylon cords are more durable and have a slight sheen. Cotton cords are soft and lightweight, making them ideal for delicate projects, while satin cords have a shiny finish that adds a touch of elegance.

Another important factor to consider is the thickness of the cord. Kumihimo cords come in various thicknesses, ranging from thin and delicate to thick and chunky. The thickness you choose will depend on the design you have in mind and the type of project you're working on. Thinner cords are often used for intricate patterns and smaller projects, while thicker cords are better suited for larger and more statement-making pieces.

The color of the cord is also an important consideration. Kumihimo cords come in a wide range of colors, allowing you to create designs that are as vibrant or as subtle as you desire. The color you choose will depend on your personal preference and the overall aesthetic you're trying to achieve. It's worth noting that some cords are dyed, while others are naturally colored. Dyed cords offer a wider range of color options, while naturally colored cords have a more organic and earthy feel.

Lastly, it's important to consider the quality of the cord. The quality of the cord will greatly impact the durability and longevity of your finished project. Look for cords that are well-made and have a tight and even braid. Avoid cords that have loose threads or frayed ends, as these can affect the overall appearance and strength of your design.

In conclusion, choosing the right Kumihimo cord is an important step in creating a beautiful and successful project. Consider the material, thickness, color, and quality of the cord to ensure that it aligns with your vision and meets your needs. With the right cord, you'll be able to create stunning Kumihimo designs that are sure to impress.

Selecting Beads and Embellishments of Kumihimo: When it comes to selecting beads and embellishments for your Kumihimo projects, there are a few factors to consider in order to achieve the desired look and feel. Kumihimo is a traditional Japanese braiding technique that involves weaving together strands of cord to create intricate patterns and designs. Adding beads and embellishments to your Kumihimo creations can elevate them to a whole new level of beauty and uniqueness.

First and foremost, it is important to choose beads and embellishments that are compatible with the Kumihimo technique. The size and shape of the beads should be suitable for threading onto the cords used in Kumihimo braiding. It is recommended to use beads with larger holes, such as seed beads or Czech glass beads, as they are easier to thread onto the cords. Additionally, beads with irregular shapes or textures can add an interesting dimension to your Kumihimo designs.

Another aspect to consider is the color scheme of your Kumihimo project. Beads and embellishments come in a wide range of colors, so you have the freedom to choose a palette that complements your overall design. You can opt for a monochromatic look by using beads in varying shades of the same color, or create a vibrant and eye-catching piece by incorporating beads in contrasting colors. It is also worth considering the color of the cords you are using, as they will influence the overall appearance of your Kumihimo creation.

In addition to color, the material of the beads and embellishments can also play a role in the final outcome of your Kumihimo project. Beads made from different materials, such as glass, metal, or gemstones, can add a touch of elegance or a rustic charm to your design. Similarly, embellishments like charms, pendants, or tassels can enhance the overall aesthetic of your Kumihimo piece. It is important to choose materials that are durable and will withstand the wear and tear of everyday use.

Furthermore, the placement of beads and embellishments within your Kumihimo design can greatly impact the overall look. You can choose to incorporate beads sporadically throughout the braid, creating a subtle and delicate effect. Alternatively, you can opt for a more intricate design by adding beads in a specific pattern or sequence. Experimenting with different placement techniques can help you achieve the desired visual impact.

Setting Up Your Kumihimo Workspace: Setting up your Kumihimo workspace is an essential step in ensuring a smooth and enjoyable braiding experience. By creating a dedicated area for your Kumihimo projects, you can easily access all the necessary tools and materials, maintain organization, and minimize distractions. In this guide, we will provide you with a comprehensive overview of how to set up your Kumihimo workspace effectively.

First and foremost, you need to find a suitable location for your Kumihimo workspace. Ideally, it should be a well-lit area with enough space to accommodate your braiding board or disk, as well as other tools and materials. Consider setting up your workspace near a window or using a bright desk lamp to ensure proper lighting, as this will help you see the intricate details of your braids more clearly.

Next, gather all the essential tools and materials you will need for your Kumihimo projects. These include a braiding board or disk, bobbins, scissors, weights, and various types of cords or threads. It's important to have these items readily available and organized within your workspace to avoid wasting time searching for them during your braiding sessions.

To keep your workspace organized, consider investing in storage solutions such as small bins, drawers, or a pegboard. These can help you categorize and store your tools and materials efficiently, making it easier to find what you need when you need it. Labeling each storage container can also be helpful, especially if you have a large collection of cords or threads.

Additionally, having a comfortable and ergonomic setup is crucial for long braiding sessions. Ensure that your chair provides adequate support for your back and that your work surface is at a comfortable height. You may want to consider using a cushion or mat to provide extra comfort for your wrists and elbows, as repetitive braiding motions can strain these areas over time.

Another important aspect of setting up your Kumihimo workspace is considering the safety of your materials and tools. If you have pets or young children, it's essential to keep your workspace out of their reach to prevent any accidents or damage to your projects. Consider using storage containers with lids or investing in a dedicated cabinet or shelf to keep your materials secure.

Lastly, personalizing your workspace can help create a pleasant and inspiring environment for your Kumihimo projects. Consider adding decorative elements such as plants, artwork, or motivational quotes to make your workspace feel inviting and enjoyable. You can also display finished braids or samples to showcase your progress and inspire creativity.

Traditional Kumihimo Braids: Round and Flat: Traditional Kumihimo braids are a type of braiding technique that originated in Japan. These braids can be created in two different styles: round and flat.

Round Kumihimo braids are created by using a round disk or a marudai, which is a traditional Japanese braiding stand. The round disk has slots around the edge, where the threads are placed. The threads are then moved in a specific pattern, crossing over each other to create the braid. This technique allows for the creation of intricate and symmetrical designs. Round Kumihimo braids are commonly used for decorative purposes, such as jewelry making or as embellishments on clothing and accessories.

On the other hand, flat Kumihimo braids are created using a rectangular disk or a takadai, which is another type of braiding stand. The rectangular disk has long, narrow slots where the threads are placed. The threads are then moved in a specific pattern, similar to the round Kumihimo braids, but with a slight variation. This technique creates a flat, ribbon-like braid that is often used for belts, straps, or decorative trims on garments.

Both round and flat Kumihimo braids can be made using various types of threads or cords, such as silk, cotton, or synthetic materials. The choice of thread can greatly impact the final appearance and texture of the braid. Additionally, different colors and patterns can be incorporated into the braid by using multiple threads of different colors or by adding beads or other embellishments.

Creating Kumihimo braids requires patience and precision, as the threads need to be carefully manipulated to achieve the desired pattern. The braiding process can be time-consuming, especially for more complex designs, but the end result is a beautiful and unique braid that showcases the artistry and craftsmanship of the braider.

In conclusion, traditional Kumihimo braids are a versatile and intricate braiding technique that can be created in round or flat styles. These braids are commonly used for decorative purposes and can be made using various types of threads and cords. The process of creating Kumihimo braids requires skill and attention to detail, but the end result is a stunning braid that showcases the beauty of this traditional Japanese craft.

Understanding Kumihimo Patterns and Designs: Kumihimo is a traditional Japanese braiding technique that has been practiced for centuries. It involves the interlacing of strands of thread or cord to create intricate and beautiful patterns. Understanding Kumihimo patterns and designs is essential for anyone interested in mastering this art form.

One of the first things to understand about Kumihimo patterns is the structure of the braiding disk or marudai. The braiding disk is a round or square foam or wooden board with slots or notches around the edge. These slots are used to hold the strands of thread or cord in place as the braiding process takes place. The marudai, on the other hand, is a stand with a central post and weighted bobbins that are used to hold the strands of thread or cord. Both the braiding disk and marudai are used in Kumihimo braiding, and understanding how to use them is crucial for creating intricate patterns.

Once you have a good understanding of the tools used in Kumihimo braiding, it is important to learn about the different types of patterns and designs that can be created. There are various types of Kumihimo patterns, including round, flat, and square braids. Each type of braid creates a different look and can be used for different purposes. Round braids are commonly used for jewelry making, while flat braids are often used for belts or straps. Square braids, on the other hand, are ideal for creating intricate patterns and designs.

To create different patterns and designs in Kumihimo braiding, different color combinations and thread arrangements can be used. By changing the order of the threads or cords and using different colors, you can create unique and eye-catching designs. It is important to experiment with different color combinations and thread arrangements to see what works best for the desired pattern or design.

In addition to color combinations and thread arrangements, the thickness and texture of the threads or cords used can also affect the final pattern or design. Thicker threads or cords will create a bolder and more pronounced pattern, while thinner threads or cords will create a more delicate and intricate design. It is important to consider the desired outcome and choose the appropriate threads or cords accordingly.

Understanding Kumihimo patterns and designs also involves learning about the different techniques used in the braiding process. There are various techniques, such as the basic 8-strand braid, the spiral braid, and the square braid, among others.

Adding Beads and Creating Patterns of Kumihimo: Kumihimo is a traditional Japanese braiding technique that involves the use of a special loom called a marudai. This technique allows you to create intricate and beautiful patterns by adding beads to your braids. By incorporating beads into your Kumihimo designs, you can add texture, color, and dimension to your finished pieces.

To begin adding beads to your Kumihimo braid, you will need to gather the necessary materials. This includes a marudai loom, Kumihimo bobbins, beading thread, beads of your choice, and a beading needle. It is important to choose beads that have a hole large enough to accommodate the beading thread and that are compatible with the size of your Kumihimo bobbins.

Once you have your materials ready, you can start by setting up your marudai loom. This involves attaching the Kumihimo bobbins to the loom and arranging them in a specific pattern. The pattern you choose will determine the placement of the beads in your braid. You can create simple or complex patterns depending on your skill level and desired outcome.

Next, you will need to thread your beads onto the beading thread using a beading needle. It is important to thread the beads in the order specified by your chosen pattern. This will ensure that the beads are placed correctly in your braid. You can experiment with different bead colors and sizes to create unique and eye-catching designs.

Once your beads are threaded onto the beading thread, you can begin braiding. To do this, you will need to follow the traditional Kumihimo braiding technique, which involves crossing the threads in a specific order. As you braid, the beads will be incorporated into the design, creating a stunning pattern. It is important to maintain tension on the threads to ensure a tight and even braid.

As you continue braiding, you will need to periodically add more beads to the beading thread. This can be done by threading the beads onto the beading thread and then continuing with the braiding process. By adding beads at regular intervals, you can create a consistent and balanced pattern throughout your braid.

Once you have completed your Kumihimo braid with the desired number of beads, you can finish off the ends by tying knots or using a clasp. This will secure the beads in place and create a finished look.

Making Kumihimo Gifts for Birthdays and Anniversaries: Kumihimo, a traditional Japanese braiding technique, has gained popularity worldwide for its intricate designs and versatility. It is not only a beautiful form of art but also a meaningful way to create personalized gifts for birthdays and anniversaries.

When it comes to gift-giving, finding something unique and special can be a challenge. However, making Kumihimo gifts allows you to create one-of-a-kind pieces that are sure to be cherished by your loved ones. The process of making Kumihimo involves weaving together different strands of thread or cord to create intricate patterns and designs. This allows you to customize the gift according to the recipient's preferences, making it truly personal and thoughtful.

One of the advantages of making Kumihimo gifts is the wide range of materials and colors available. You can choose from various types of threads, cords, and beads to create a design that matches the recipient's style and personality. Whether they prefer vibrant and bold colors or subtle and elegant tones, you can easily find the perfect materials to bring your vision to life.

Furthermore, Kumihimo gifts can be tailored to suit any occasion. For birthdays, you can create bracelets, necklaces, or keychains with the recipient's birthstone incorporated into the design. This adds a touch of personalization and symbolism to the gift, making it even more meaningful. For anniversaries, you can create matching sets for couples, such as his and hers bracelets or necklaces, symbolizing their bond and love for each other.

The process of making Kumihimo gifts is not only enjoyable but also therapeutic. As you weave the threads together, you can find a sense of calm and relaxation. It allows you to disconnect from the stresses of everyday life and focus on creating something beautiful. This makes it a perfect hobby for those looking for a creative outlet or a way to unwind after a long day.

Additionally, Kumihimo gifts are not limited to jewelry. You can also create decorative items such as bookmarks, coasters, or even wall hangings. These unique pieces can add a touch of elegance and charm to any home or office space. They serve as a constant reminder of the special occasion and the thought and effort put into creating the gift.

In conclusion, making Kumihimo gifts for birthdays and anniversaries is a wonderful way to show your loved ones how much you care. The intricate designs, personalized touch, and therapeutic process make these gifts truly special.

Kumihimo for Home Decor: Kumihimo is a traditional Japanese braiding technique that has been used for centuries to create beautiful and intricate designs. While it is often associated with jewelry making, Kumihimo can also be used to create stunning home decor pieces.

One of the most popular ways to incorporate Kumihimo into home decor is by using it to create decorative cords. These cords can be used in a variety of ways, such as curtain tiebacks, lampshade trims, or even as a decorative element on furniture. The intricate patterns and vibrant colors of Kumihimo cords can add a unique and eye-catching touch to any room.

Another way to use Kumihimo for home decor is by creating wall hangings or tapestries. By braiding together different colors and textures of yarn or thread, you can create a stunning piece of art that can be hung on a wall or used as a room divider. The versatility of Kumihimo allows you to experiment with different patterns and designs, making each piece truly one-of-a-kind.

Kumihimo can also be used to create decorative accents for furniture or home accessories. By braiding together thin strips of fabric or ribbon, you can create beautiful trimmings for pillows, curtains, or even table runners. These braided accents can add a touch of elegance and sophistication to any room.

In addition to its decorative uses, Kumihimo can also be functional in home decor. For example, you can use Kumihimo to create unique and personalized keychains or zipper pulls. By braiding together different colors and textures of cord, you can create a functional and stylish accessory that adds a personal touch to your everyday items.

Overall, Kumihimo is a versatile and beautiful technique that can be used to create stunning home decor pieces. Whether you choose to incorporate it into your curtains, furniture, or accessories, Kumihimo adds a unique and artistic touch to any room. So why not try your hand at this ancient Japanese art form and create your own beautiful Kumihimo home decor?

CHAPTER ONE

GETTING STARTED WITH KUMIHIMO

What is Kumihimo?

Kumi himo is a Japanese term that translates as ''gathered threads''. It is the art of braiding cords, threads, ribbons, strands of beads, and jewelry wire into beautiful ropes. These ropes, also known as kumihimo, are strong yet slim and versatile.

History of Kumihimo

Kumihimo is an old skill dating all the way back to the sixth century. The old art forms stretch all the way back to well over 1300 years. Due to the perishable nature of braid materials and the secrecy surrounding braiding techniques, the early history of Kumihimo is difficult to study. Not until around 400 years ago were braid designs published.

Kumihimo braids have been utilized in a variety of ways throughout Japanese history. Buddhism introduced braiding to Japan, where it was used in clothing and rituals. Kumihimo braids were later heavily used into Samurai armor and weapons, as well as kimono attire.

The obi, the traditional belt of the kimono, was traditionally wrapped with a kumihimo string called an obijime. It is a work of art that is both culturally relevant and aesthetically pleasing.

In recent history, the art has had a regeneration because to Makiko Tada's development of the foam Kumihimo disk and plate.

Initially, the operation was carried out totally by hand, without the use of any instrument. Generally, the early kumihimo are monochromatic or have a very restricted color palette.

Later on, weavers developed tools that let them to create more complex patterns, allowing producers to use additional colors. The original kumihimo looms, known as takadai and marudai, are somewhat huge and heavy, as well as quite immovable.

What is kumihimo Used for?

Kumihimo was originally used to embellish Buddhist scrolls and other religious items. They were subsequently used to connect Samurai armour and Kimonos.

While they are still used to decorate sacred artifacts and kimonos, they are also available as necklaces, bracelets, and even wall art. Kumihimo works became famous as tourist gifts due to their trendy and sophisticated presentation of a traditional Japanese art method.

Additionally, in recent years, an increasing number of individuals have gravitated into Kumihimo in search of opportunities to produce their own works. From friendship bracelets to necklaces, from bags to wall art, the sight and feel of Kumihimo creations captivates the public.

Different shapes and patterns may be created by modifying the braiding material, the thickness or number of strands, the shape of the disk against the square plate, and by adding beads to your kumihimo braid.

Kumihimo can withstand a great deal of wear and tear due to the fact that it is made up of several strands of robust and resilient silk. It produces a strange yet durable dog leash, handbag strap, or belt. The process of weaving kumihimo from several strands allows for an infinite number of color combinations.

CHAPTER TWO

TOOLS USED FOR KUMIHIMO

As is the case with other favorite beading methods, kumihimo may be done with an almost infinite number of materials. Before you begin your first beaded kumihimo project, ensure that you have a few essential items on available to ensure a satisfactory outcome. We'll go over all of the kumihimo braiding materials you'll need to get started with this great hobby in this section.

Kumihimo Disks

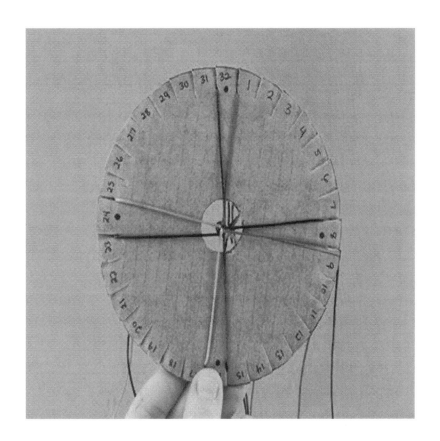

In the beading world, a disk is utilized for Kumihimo. For novices, foam kumihimo disks are ideal. They're inexpensive, you can write on them to indicate your location, and they're lightweight and extremely portable. Disks come in a variety of forms and sizes, depending on the kind of project you're working on.

kumihimo disks are available in two shapes: round and square. Circular foam kumihimo disks in 6″ and 4″ sizes are often used to create round braids with a hollow central core. To create a flat braid suited for a flat bracelet, a square kumihimo disk is utilized.

Additionally, you may purchase disks in a variety of sizes. This has no effect on the completed braid. However, you may discover that you are more at ease with bigger disks — or with smaller disks. This is very dependent on the size of your hands and how you hold your work. As a result, the size is irrelevant when you first begin. However, as you gain skill, you may like to experiment with other sizes.

You'll notice that the disks are numbered and include a hole in the center. What you probably cannot see as well are the grooved edges.

As a result, when you configure the disk, you will be prompted to thread your wire through precise numbered grooves. Because the cords cross in the center, the braided cord will flow downward through the central hole as you braid.

Kumihimo Bobbins

Bobbins were the other essential Kumihimo item that is needed. Braiding consumes a significant amount of cable. Thus, even if you're making a bracelet for a little wrist, you'll need an extremely lengthy piece of string.

While you work, all of your wires will be dangling from the disk's outside border. As a result, if you leave them hanging free, they will quickly get tangled as you move the cords about to construct the braid.

That is where bobbins come into play . A set of plastic bobbins is required to handle the many strands and to secure any beads in place when braiding. Each cable may be wound onto a bobbin. Thus, instead of large lengths of thread, you now have bobbins dangling from the borders of your disk. Simply unwind the line as needed, and tangled cords are a thing of the past!.

The good thing about all of this is that the bobbins and even the weight may be used in a variety of different craft projects. There are different sizes of bobbins available. Thus, even if your rope has beads, you can still wound everything into a bobbin to avoid tangles!

Again, as a general guideline, ensure that your collection of beading materials includes one pair of bobbins for each foam loom.Try to maintain one pair of bobbins for each foam kumihimo disc in your beading equipment collection so that you may work on many projects concurrently.

Weights

As you work, your braid will drop through the disk's core hole so having a weight to lead it through is quite beneficial. Additionally, this assists you in achieving a more balanced tension. You may use a homemade objec as a beginner. However, it is advisable to get a weight as you get used to the craft to make your work fast and easy.

Kumihimo Weight
www.myworldofbeads.com

Attach the weight to your combined cables at their point of intersection, in the center of the disk's hole. As you work, the weight hangs below and will continue to draw your finished braid down.

Kumihimo Cord

There are several cable alternatives to choose from when creating a kumihimo braid, both with and without beads.

If you're building a kumihimo braid using large-hole beads I'd recommend using a little thinner cable to ensure that all eight strands pass through the center hole of the focal bead.

To highlight a focal bead or a unique pair of end caps, you may use satin rat tail cord in thicknesses ranging from 0.5mm to 3mm. The vibrant hues of these silky cords will result in an incredibly beautiful final kumihimo braid. However, keep in mind that a thicker satin string will cause the slots in your foam kumihimo discs to enlarge.

Another excellent material for kumihimo braids is leather cord. Leather may be utilized to create both men's and women's kumihimo jewelry, as well as more rustic and Bohemian-style pieces.

Kumihimo end caps and claps

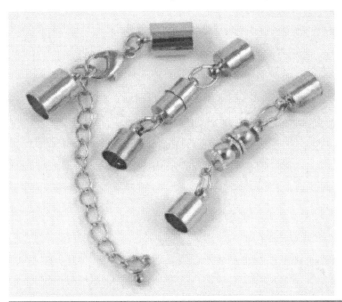

White Silver

Decorative end caps may be used to cover the ends of your kumihimo braids, depending on your personal preference. End caps are available in a wide range of forms, metals, and colors, ranging from very big to extremely tiny.

Kumihimo Beads

Some may say that the beads are the most appealing aspect of beaded kumihimo—and I would agree! And here is when the real fun begins: selecting your kumihimo bead material. Your completed creation will be uniquely yours due to the beads!

A few tubes of size 6 seed beads is sufficient for starting beaded kumihimo projects. Once you've mastered the art of beading your kumihimo braids, explore with 3mm fire-polished glass beads, 3mm round glass druks, lightweight gemstone beads, pearls, or even antique German and Czech glass beads. For maximum glitz, invest in crystal beads or stock up on affordable Chinese crystals to create gorgeous beaded kumihimo ropes right out of the 1920s.

Kumihimo Loom

The Kumi Loom disc itself makes kumihimo weaving a very relaxing pastime. The notches around the loom's outside edge are numbered, and the weaver inserts a silken strand into them. Another strand is taken in by a notch on the other side, and so on until all strands are in place. The weaving then starts.

Weaving kumihimo is as easy as counting using the KumiLoom. To begin, the weaver inserts a silk strand into the slot below and to the right. Following that, the direction is upward and to the left. Finally, the whole loom receives a left turn. It's astonishing that this simple three-step method can result in such intricate designs as kumihimo.

Guidelines for kumihimo Weaving

The following are the most fundamental guidelines you should be aware of.

• To straighten curly nylon cables, gently steam them. This will significantly simplify the process of stringing your beads.

• String beads onto the cords using a large-eye needle. Alternatively, you may dip the cord ends in Super Glue gel and let to dry to thread beads without the need of a needle.

• Slit a 12" slit on the rear of each bobbin to secure the cord ends.

Using a kumihimo stand enables you to braid with both hands, rather as holding your disk in one hand and stringing beads and braiding with the other. Your tension will be more consistent, and the overall appearance of your product will be more professional. Additionally, if you are interrupted, a kumihimo stand provides a tangle-free method to store your creation.

• If you are stopped during the braiding process, just shift the bottom-left cord to the top position and leave it there. You'll have three cords at the top position, and you'll always know precisely where to restart your project. When you restart, pull the top right cable down, quarter-turn the disk, and continue.

• Note on gauge: Not all beads are made equal! While the gauge for size 8° seed beads is typically 6 per braided inch, this formula will not always work. The only way to determine if a certain color or finish will work with this recipe is to do a test braid. Take note of any required adjustments to gauge and make any adjustments to your design.

CHAPTER THREE

HOW TO BEGIN WITH KUMIHIMO

Basic Round Braid with 8 Warps

This method involves the use of a variety of looms to create a variety of braids. This lesson demonstrates a simple circular braid with eight warps.

When practicing Kumihimo, you will discover that varying the quantity of strands and the color of the strands alters the overall appearance. Changing the stringing material and adding beads to all or portion of the strands may also alter the appearance. Bear in mind that you may not want to use a stretchy stringing material.

Each thread in a single "slit" is referred to as a warp in Kumihimo. We'll be using a round Kumihimo disk with 32 slots to make an eight-warp basic round braid in this tutorial. When gauging stringing material, a decent rule of thumb is to multiply the desired length by three. This will work for the majority of designs, unless you are using bigger beads, in which case the length may need to be adjusted. After you've mastered the basic circle braid, learn how to embellish Kumihimo with beads.

INSTRUCTIONS

Step One -Setting up the Disk

Gather all eight strands and secure one end with a knot. If you're working with extra-long lengths, we recommend utilizing bobbins to prevent tangling.

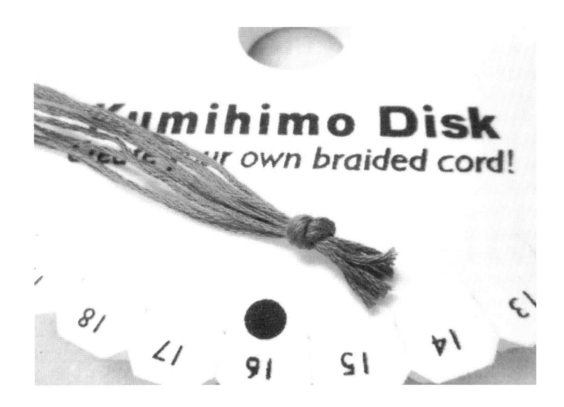

Step two

Insert the knotted end into the Kumihimo disk's center hole.

Step three

Divide the strands into four groups of two and put them over the disk at the black location marks. When configuring the disk, place the number 32 at the top.

Step Four

Begin with 32 strands and lay one on either side of the dot. Pull the threads gently into the slits.

Step Five

Cross the disk straight across and insert one thread into each slit on each side of the black dot on the number 16. Maintain sufficient strain on the strands to keep the knot in the middle of the disk's hole.

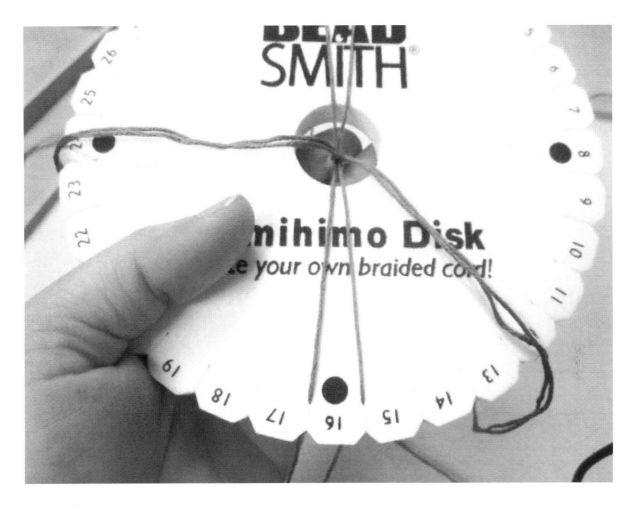

Step Six

At the right of the disk, insert one strand into each of the openings on each side of the black dot on the number 8.

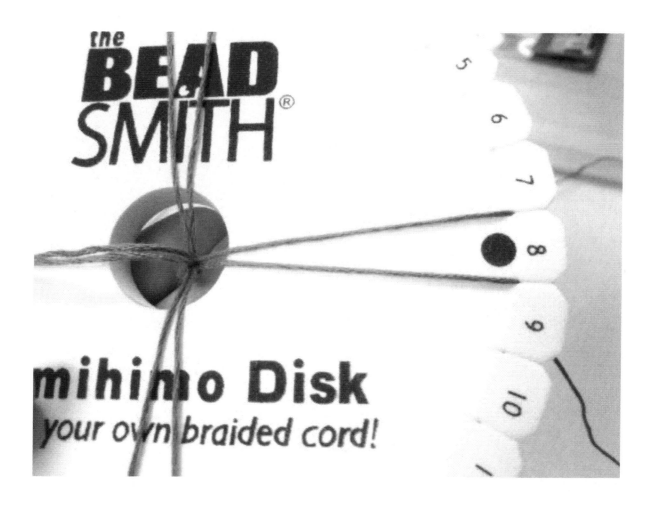

Step Seven

Proceed to the disk's left side and insert one strand into each of the slits on each side of this black dot on number 24. After you've secured all of the cables, your disk should look like this. Keep in mind that the knot remains centered.

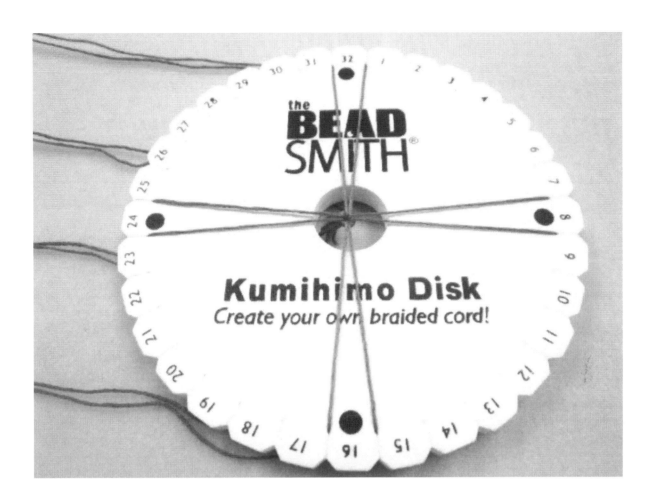

Beginning The Braid

Please keep in mind that when we refer to a numbered slit, we are referring to the slit immediately to the left of that number.

You may want to retain some weight behind the knot at the disk's center, particularly at the beginning of the braid, to maintain a tight, consistent appearance as you go. You may accomplish this by hand, holding the knot end and gradually pushing down as you go, but it may be quicker to secure the knot using a tiny bag containing twenty-five cents. This allows both hands to be used for braiding.

Step Eight

Begin by extending the rope in split 17 straight up and over the disk

to slit 31.

Step Nine: Continue over the disk with cable 1 until you reach slit 15. Bear in mind to maintain the same amount of tension throughout the braid to ensure an even braid free of bumps.

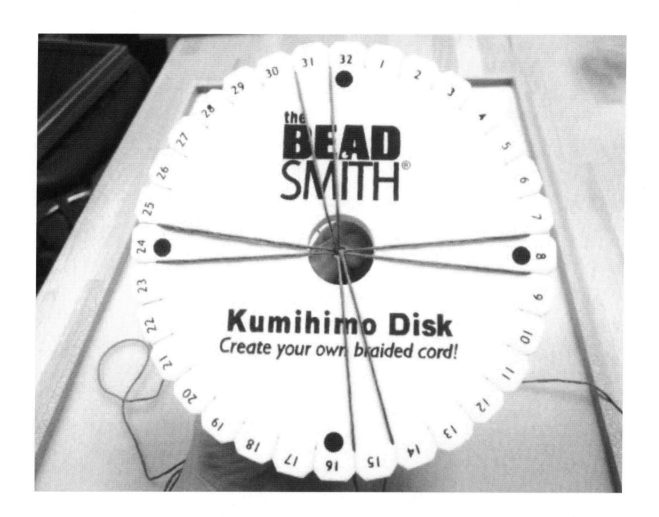

Step Ten: Take a 1/4 turn clockwise on the Kumihimo disk. At this point, the black positioning dot at number 24 should be at the top.

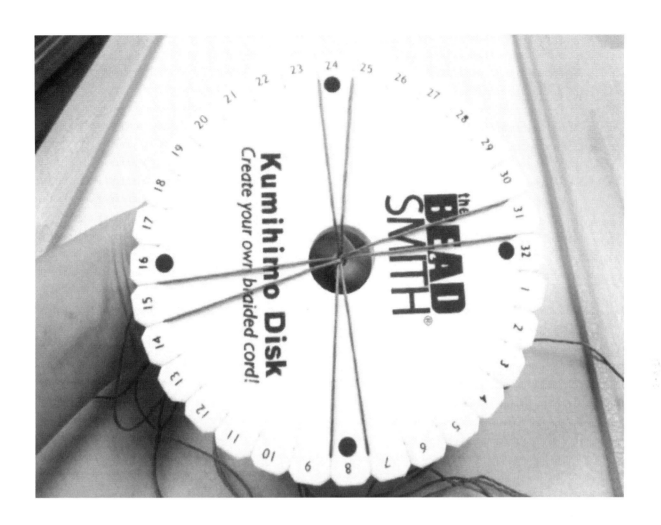

Step Eleven: Move cord 9 to slit 23 and bear in mind to maintain tension on the threads.

Step Twelve: Continue across chord 25 to slit 7.

Step Thirteen: Turn the disc one quarter clockwise to reach the next set of cables. As you can see, you are essentially repeating steps two through four for each chord combination (up and left, down and right). After a few laps around the disk, the numbers become irrelevant.

Step Fourteen: Repeat steps two through four until the desired length is obtained. The length depends depend on the design and the procedure used to finish the ends.

Step Fifteen: Remove the braid from the disk and secure the unfinished end with a knot.

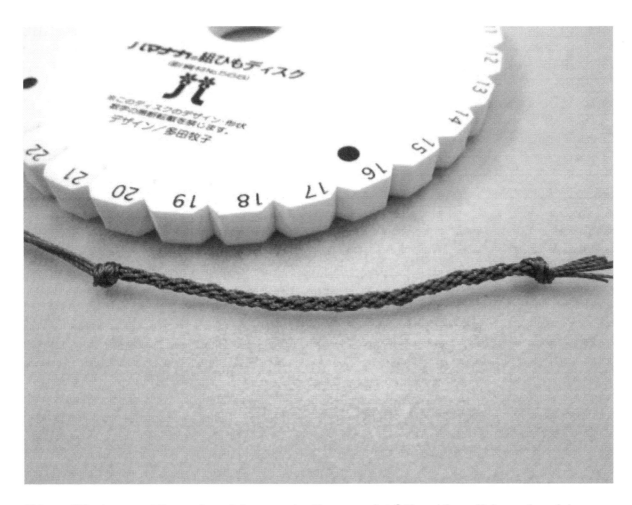

Step Sixteen: Tie a knot towards the end of the Kumihimo braid using Nymo D string.

Step Seventeen: Wrap one end of the Nymo as tightly as possible around the braid. Wrap the Nymo in the opposite direction as the initial wrap.

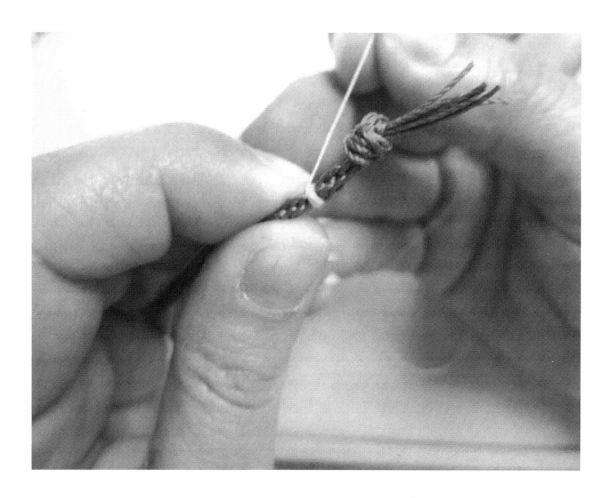

Step Eighteen: Tie another knot in the Nymo and burn the surplus thread using a thread burner.

Step Nineteen: Cut the braid's knot.

Step Twenty: Cut the end of the braid to a length that will contain your end clap. In the picture below, a crimp end with a loop is used.

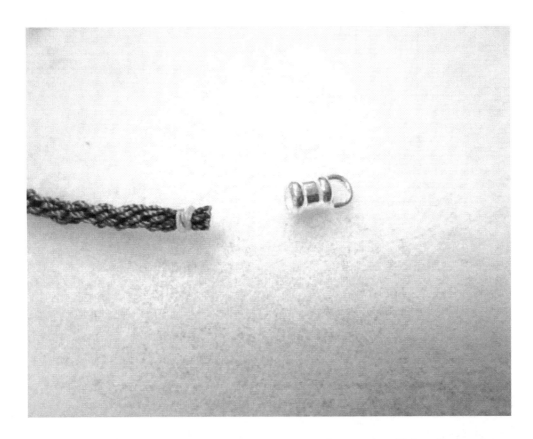

Step Twenty Three: To cover the Nymo thread, slide the crimp end over the end of the braid and crimp with a set of chain nose pliers.

Wow! Your 8 strand kumihibo spiral braid is ready. This can be use to make a beaded necklace or bracelets which will be demontrated in the next chapter.

Having known how to go about the 8 strands, lets proceed to making a 12 strand spiral kumihimo braid. Ready?

CHAPTER FOUR

Making a 12 Strand Spiral Kumihimo Braid

And, as it turns out, the spiral with 12 strands is just as simple as the 8 strands and you can make as much as four of it in a night cos it's so so simple.

Now Let's get started!

Materials and Tools You Need

- A round kumihimo disk
- 2mm Cords of different colours of your choice. The colours used in this tutorial are yellow and pink(.Yellow as the outer colour and pink as the inner colour).
- A pair of scissors

Procedures

- Make four cuttings of your inner color of about 39 inches long and two cuttings of your outer color of about 45 inches long.

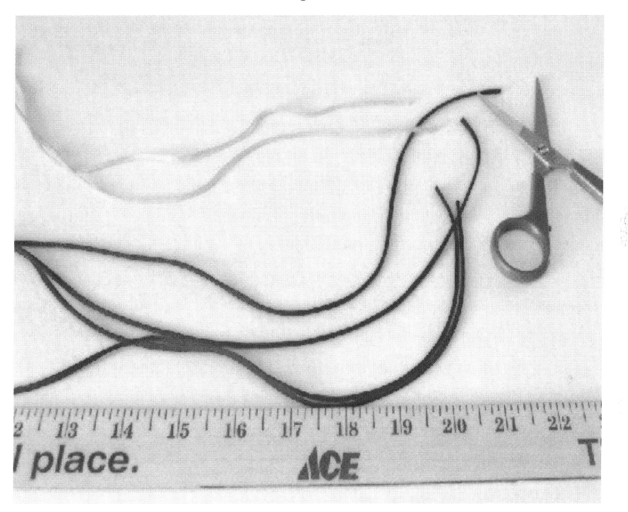

- Put the ends of the cords together and locate the center. Then and secure with a strong knot.

- Pass the knot through the front of the disk.

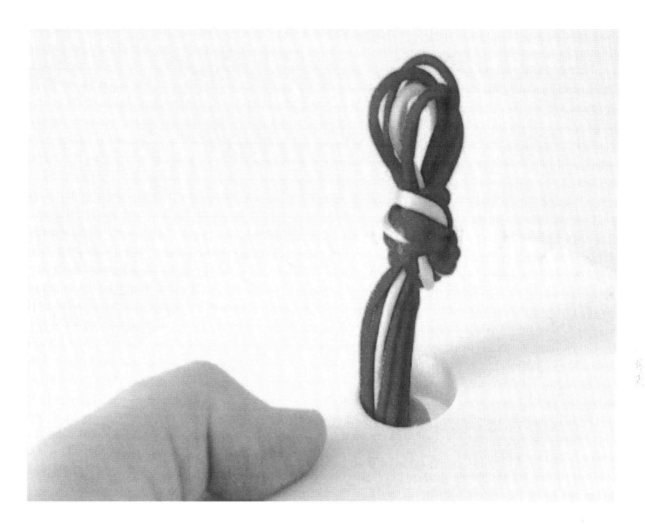

- Lace the disk as shown below

Let the inner colour go on each side of the disk marked 2, 14, 18, and 30.

While the outer colour will go on each side of disk marked 8 and 24.

We're going to split the disk in half horizontally, left and right.

- Take the bottom left chord and put it to the left of the top left cord on the left side.
- Place the top right cable to the right of the bottom left cord.
- Take the cable on the bottom left and put it to the left of the top left chord on the right side.

- Place the top right chord to the right of the bottom right cable left.
- Rotate the disk and reposition the bottom left cable to the left of the top left chord.
- Place the top right cable to the right of the sole cord remaining on the bottom.
- Turn the disk and repeat the pattern.

Your cable will begin to emerge from the rear as you work the disk.

When you've reached the desired length, grasp all of the cords and squeeze them together to prevent them from unraveling on you and remove it carefully from the disk.

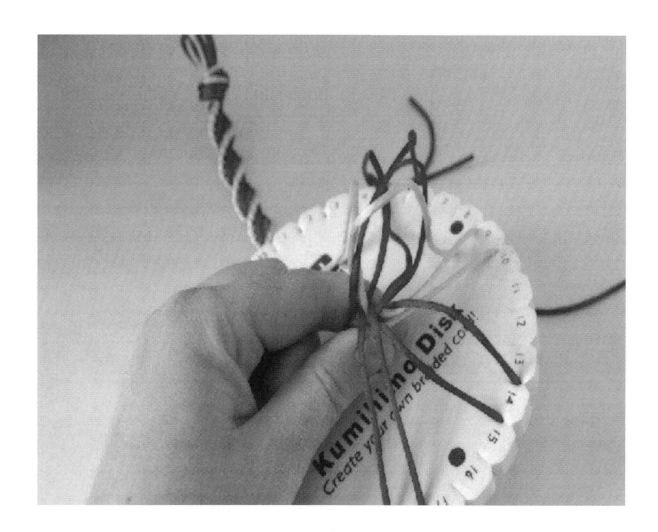

- Secure the end with a knot.

- Tie the ends through the knot, similar to how you would with a standard friendship bracelet.
- Bonded the knot in place ensuring that glue is placed both within and around the knot and make sure that the glue dries clearly.

Take the raw ends and ignite them with a lighter. It just takes a split second, but this will secure the ends and prevent them from unraveling.Make sure that the cord is not flammable.

Due to the fact that the knots are bounded in place, you can wear it as a bangle and just put it on your wrist.

I hope you had fun going through this tutorial.

Do well to experiment it with different colours and see the beauty of it.

Up next is the making of flat braid Kumihimo.

CHAPTER FIVE

HOW TO MAKE FLAT BRAID KUMIHIMO

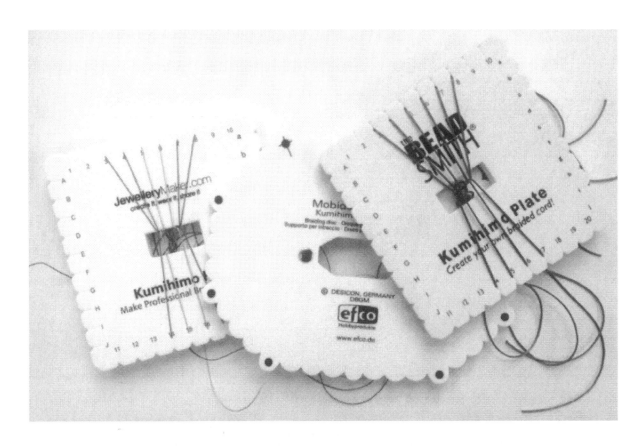

10 Cord Flat Braid with a Chevron Design

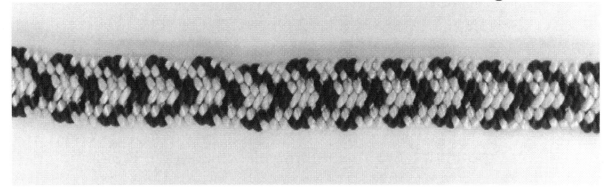

This is the most often used flat braid design since it is simple to learn and results in a functional flat braid. By alternating colors, you may make V and X-shaped shapes in the braid. This may also be created with 14 or 18 cords, however maintaining a uniform tension would be more challenging with that many cords.

Getting Started

- Insert six cords into slots 3,4,5,6,7, and 8 on the top of the disk; and then four cords in slots 14,15,16, and 17 on the bottom of the disk.

- Remove the cord in slot 5 and place it in slot e and the also the cord in slot 6 to slot E.

- Begin with the wires on the left side of the plate. Carry out the following movements of cords:15 to 5, 4 to15, 14 to 4, and 3 to 14

- Then on the right side of the plate, carry out the following movements of cords: 16 to 6, 7 to16, 17 to 7,

and 8 to 17

- Transfer the cord from slot E to slot 3 then from slot e to slot 8.

This will bring the cords back to their initial position. Then continue with the steps shown above until the braid reaches the length you desire.

It is advisable to practice this braid numerous times before commencing on a specific piece of jewelry, since equal tension is necessary for the braid to have straight edges. The transitions from 5 to e and 6 to E are critical because they determine the breadth of the braid. The more they are drawn up, the finer the braid becomes. Consistency in these movements results in an equal breadth and straight sides.

It's enjoyable to play with various color placements to produce different results.

CHAPTER SIX

MAKING KUMIHIMO WITH BEADS

Once you've mastered the fundamentals of creating a Kumihimo braid, you'll almost certainly want to experiment with adding beads to the braid. This requires a bit more preparation time before you begin, but the results are well worth the effort. When developing your design, take in mind that the ultimate product will vary according to the color scheme, the size of the beads, and the number of beaded strands used. Additionally, keep in mind that the stringing material size will be decided by the hole size of the beads you want to use.

Instructions to Making a beaded 8 Strand circular kumihimo

- Determine the desired length of braid first. As a general guideline, cut the stringing material three times the required length. This should suit the majority of designs, even those including beads.
- Following that, you'll need to establish the quantity of beads required. On all eight strands, we're using TOHO beads in size 8/0.

Then, proceed with the following steps:

#1: String one bead and then work your way back up through it to make a stopper bead. Do this procedure for all eight strands.

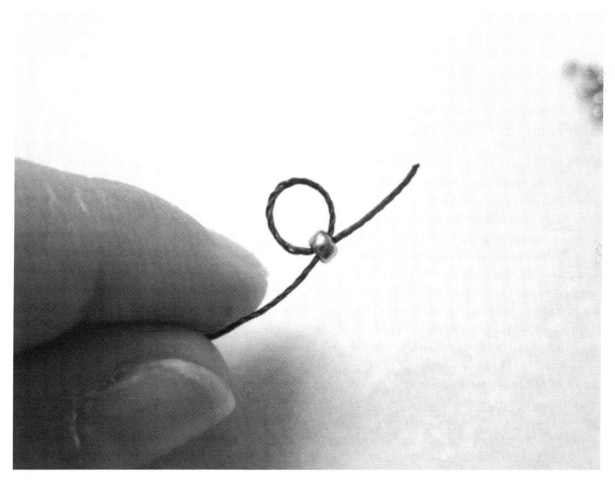

#2: String the required number of beads onto each thread. Then wind each strand of beads onto its own bobbin, leaving the open stringing end exposed.

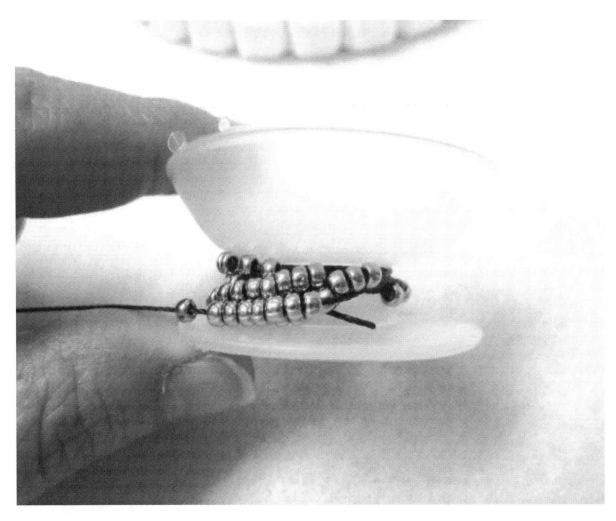

#3: Tie all the eight strands open stringing ends together in a knot.

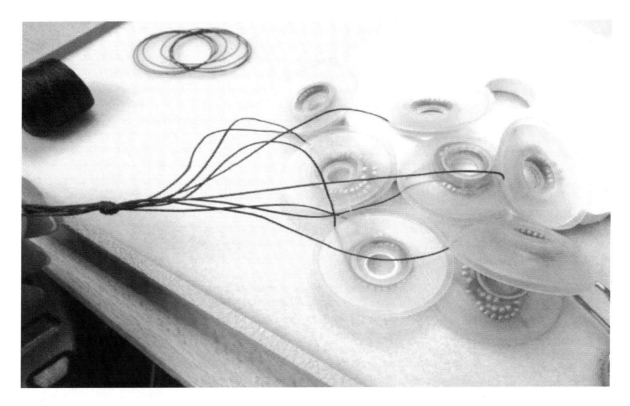

 # 4: Place the knot in the Kumihimo disk's center hole and the strings in the slots on each side of the placement dots.

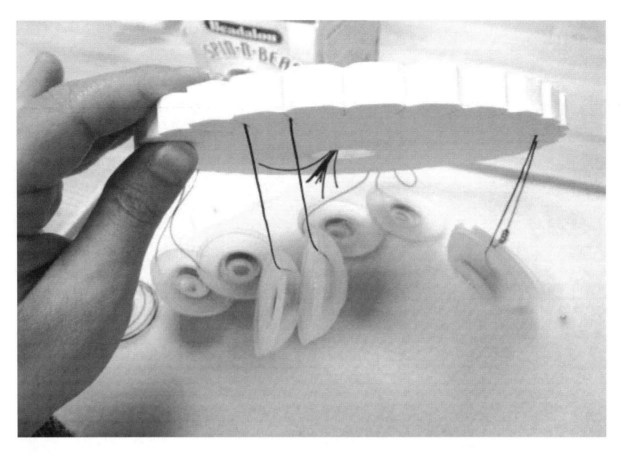

This is how your Kumihimo disk should appear.

 # 5: Braid about half inch of braid without adding beads. Without beads in this portion, it will be simpler to tie the end when it comes time to complete the braid.

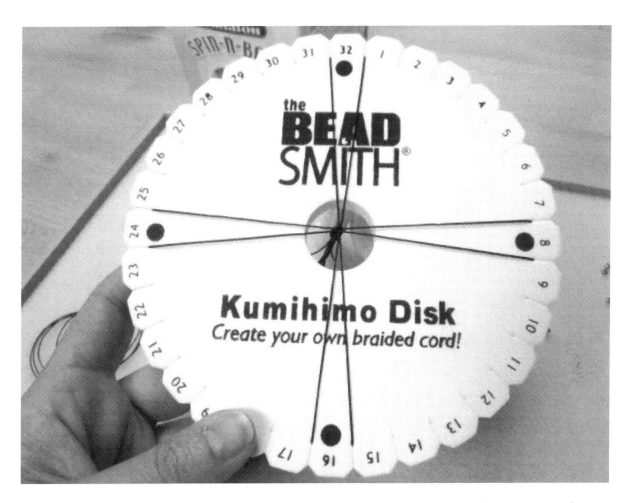

 # 6: Take a few beads from each bobbin and thread them onto the strands, then shut the bobbins.

Braiding instructions are same whether beads are used or not. The only difference is that if you're using beads, you'll need to insert one bead into the braid for each strand as you go. Take note that the first few beads may seem jumbled. They should balance out as you advance as long as you remember to maintain proper string tension while working.

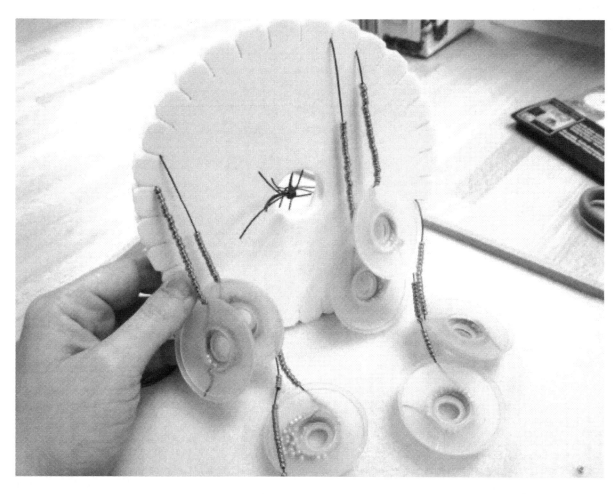

 # 8: Extricate warp 17 from the slit and thread one bead onto the string. Slide the bead as far as possible.Make sure it rests under warp 24.

 # 9: Raise warp 17 and insert it into slit 31.

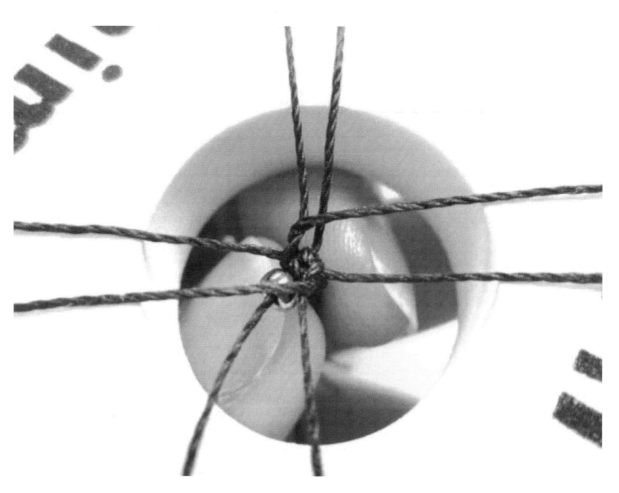

 # 10: slid up one bead onto warp 1 and let it rest under wrap 8.

 # 11: Reduce warp 1 to slit 15.

#12: Turn the Kumihimo disk one quater turn clockwise, or 90 degrees, until the dot between slots 8 and 9 is on the bottom. Then bring one bead onto warp 9 until it is positioned under warp 15.

#13:Remove warp 9 and place it in slit 23.

#14: Bring 1 bead up onto warp 25 to continue this design. Drop warp 25 into slit 7 such that the bead rests just below warp 31.

#15: Make a one-quarter turn clockwise on the disk and slide 1 bead onto warp 32. Then, move warp 32 over to slit 14.

#16 :Fix 1 bead to warp 16 and move it to slit 30. Then make a clockwise one-quarter turn on the disk.

#17: Continue in this manner until the required length is obtained. Do not include the half inch of unbeaded braid in your total length, since it will be cut off.

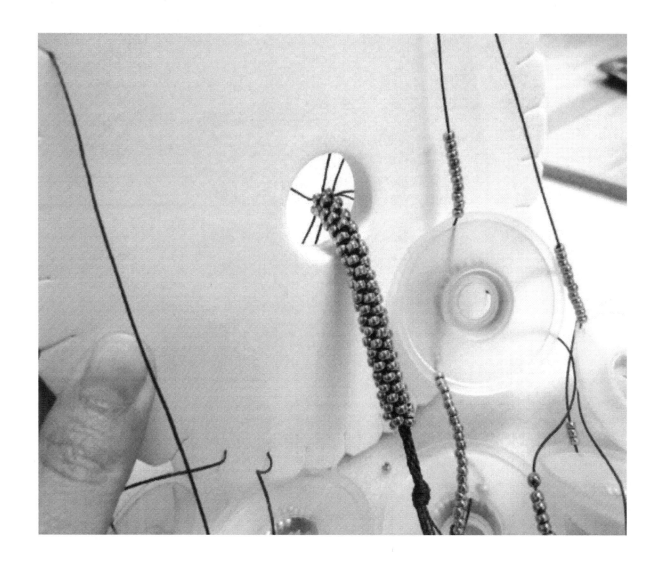

#18: Make an additional half inch of plain braid.

#19: Remove the braid from the disk and make a knot in the ends of all eight strands.

#20: To Fix a crimp at the end, cut a length of Nymo D thread and secure one end of the braid with a knot.

Wrap one end of the Nymo tightly around the braid several times and then repeat with the other end moving in the opposite direction.

Secure with another knot and then trim the extra thread with a thread

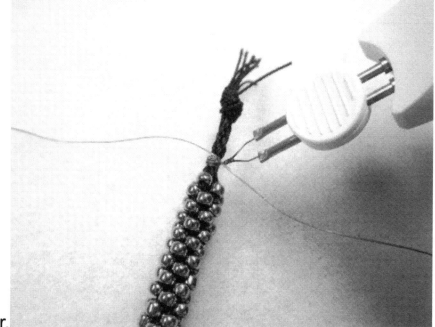

burner.

#21: Trim off the end of the braid

#22: Cover the end with a crimp end to conceal the Nymo and then crimp with a pair of chain nose pliers.

#23: To Add End Caps to a kumihimo braid, continue wrapping the braid with Nymo as instructed before. This is an excellent moment to measure the end and determine the appropriate size end cap. Bear in mind the length of the braid's end, as you want it to stretch all the way to the very tip of the endcap for a tight grasp. It is better to leave the end long and then test your end cap to ensure it fits properly. Reduce the length more if necessary until the fit is right.

#24: Apply a little amount of glue to the interior of the endcap and the braid's end and fix the endcaps on the braid ends as far as possible and then allow it to dry.

.

Here you have your beaded kumihimo which can be worn as a bracelet or a necklace depending on the length.

Conclusion

I am super sure that you find this book educating and interesting as you have learnt the basis of kumihimo. I encourage you to keep repeating the guidlines contained in this book and in no time you will be a professional in KUMIHIMO.

Cheers!

Made in United States
Orlando, FL
12 May 2024

46782844R00057